My First
Computer
Guide

Chris Oxlade

Heinemann Library

Chicago, Illinois

© 2007 Heinemann Library
a division of Reed Elsevier Inc.
Chicago, Illinois

Customer Service 888-454-2279
Visit our website at www.heinemannraintree.com

Designed by Philippa Jenkins
Illustrations by Tower Designs (UK) Ltd
Picture research by Melissa Allison
Production by Duncan Gilbert

Originated by Dot Gradations
Printed and bound in China by South China
Printing Co. Ltd

11 10 09 08 07
10 9 8 7 6 5 4 3 2 1

ISBN: 978-1-4329-0018-2 (hardcover)
       978-1-4329-0022-9 (paperback)

Library of Congress Cataloguing-in-Publication Data
Oxlade, Chris
   My First Computer Guide / Chris Oxlade.
     p. cm. -- (My First Computer Guides)
   Includes bibliographical references and index.
   ISBN 978-1-4329-0018-2 (hc)
   -- ISBN 978-1-4329-0022-9 (pb)
   1. Computers--Juvenile literature. I. Title.

QA76.23.O95 2007
004--dc22
               2006100905

Acknowledgements

The publishers would like to thank the following
for permission to reproduce photographs: Alamy
pp. **10** left (archivberlin Fotoagentur GmbH), **28**
(Charles Bowman), **5** right and **21** (ImageDJ); Apple
Computer, Inc. p. **4**; Corbis pp. **6** (LWA-Dann Tardif),
10 (Michael Prince), **19** (LWA- JDC), **27** (Royalty-
Free), **29** (Charles O'Rear); Getty Images pp. **18-19**
(Photodisc); Harcourt Education Ltd pp. **5** bottom,
6/7, **8/9**, **20**, **25** (Tudor Photography), **26** (Heinemann
Explore); Lexmark International p. **5** left; Microsoft
TM. Internet Explorer is a registered trademark
of Microsoft Corporation in the United States and
United Kingdom p. **13** left; Mozilla.org p. **13** right
and **14**; PhotoEdit Inc/Bill Aron p. **23**; Sony Europe
p. **5** top

Cover photograph of optical computer mouse,
reproduced with permission of Corbis (William
Whitehurst).

The publishers would like to thank Robert Eiffert for
his assistance in the preparation of this book.

Contents

Some words are shown in bold, **like this**. You can find out what they mean by looking in the glossary.

Learning About Computers

screen (monitor)

mouse

keyboard

A computer is a special type of machine.
It can do many different jobs.

This computer is called a laptop computer, or notebook computer.

scanner

printer

These machines plug into the computer.

camera

5

How We Use Computers

We use computers at school, at home, and at work. They help us with writing, drawing and painting, math, sending messages, and finding information.

Computers help us work on projects.

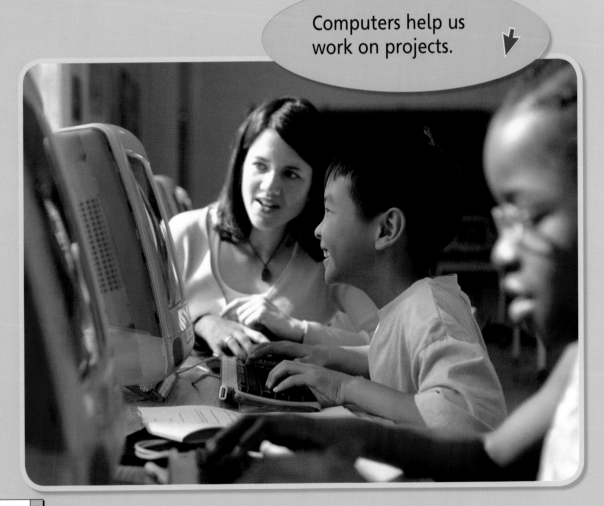

We can also use computers to store things. We can store photographs, music, and videos on a computer. Many people also use computers to play games.

On and Off

You have to press the power switch to turn a computer on before you can use it. It takes a few seconds to start up.

Registered Users:

User Name

Password

Enter

You might have to type in a password before you can start using the computer.

When you have finished using a computer, you must shut it down. You shut down the computer by clicking on a button. You do not press the power switch to turn off the computer.

When you click on the "Shut Down" button on the screen, the computer will turn itself off.

Moving a Mouse

You use the **mouse** to make the computer do things. The mouse makes a pointer move around on the screen. You can click on things and move things with the mouse.

↑ The mouse looks like a real mouse, with a long tail.

Sometimes you need one click. Sometimes you need to click twice quickly. This is called a double-click.

When you click on something and hold down the button, you can drag it across the screen.

My Story

My Story

Activity

Go to a computer and practice moving the mouse in different directions. Watch the pointer on the screen to see how it is moving.

Computer Programs

A computer **program** lets us do things with a computer. A word processor program lets us write words and sentences using the keyboard. A painting program lets us make pictures on the screen.

A painting program has buttons we can use for making a picture.

Some programs let us look at information or sort it out. Other programs let us write or speak to other people. Game programs let us play on the computer.

These programs let us look at Web sites on the Internet.

Internet Explorer   Firefox

On Your Desktop

After the computer has started up, you see the **desktop**. On the desktop are small pictures called **icons**.

This is a **program** icon. A program starts when you double-click on it.

Firefox

Home

This is a folder icon. You double-click on it to open the folder. There will be information inside it.

The button to shut down your computer is on the desktop. There is also a trash or recycling bin. You can put work you no longer need in there.

Trash

Recycle Bin

Using Windows

When you open a folder or start a **program**, a box appears on the screen. This box is called a **window**. You can have many windows open on the desktop at the same time.

You click and drag here to change the size of the window.

When you open a window, there are **menus** on the screen. These menus let you choose what you want to do. Click on your choice with the **mouse**.

Clicking here makes the menu appear.

| File | Edit | View | Insert | Format |

New Document
Open
Close
Save
Print

Your choice is highlighted with a bar of color.

Activity
To close a window down, click on the ⊠ **icon** in the top corner. Now try to hide a window without closing it. You click on the ▭ icon in the top corner.

Putting Stuff In

We put information into a computer as we work on it. The information is called **data**. We put in letters and numbers with the keyboard. Pressing keys also makes the computer do things, such as moving the page up and down.

number keys

letter keys

Press the "Shift" key to get capital letters.

Press the space bar to add spaces between words.

Press the "Delete" key to erase a letter or number.

STAY SAFE X

⚠ Always sit upright at a desk while you are using a computer. The screen and keyboard should be straight ahead of you.

More Input

There are many ways of putting **data** into a computer. The data can be stored on the computer.

A **digital camera** puts photographs into the computer. Information goes along a cable into the computer.

cable

A scanner is a machine that makes a copy of something. You can put photographs, pictures, and paintings in a scanner. The scanner turns them into information that you can store on the computer.

A computer needs a special **program** to use a scanner.

STAY SAFE X

⚠ Never unplug equipment while it is sending data to the computer. Always be gentle with equipment and cables.

Printing Out

We often want to print out the information we see on the screen. We do this with a printer. The printer makes a copy of the information on paper.

Click the "Print" button when you want to print.

Print

Click "Print" to start printing.

Always ask your teacher or another adult before you print things out. There might be rules to follow so that paper and ink are not wasted.

 STAY SAFE **X**

⚠ Take regular breaks from looking at the computer screen. This will stop your eyes from getting tired.

Saving and Opening

Always save your work before shutting down the computer. Then you can get it back later. The work is saved as a file in the computer.

Choose where you want to put the file here.

Files are stored in folders on the computer. You might have your own folder.

Save as

Look in: My Story

My Recent Documents

Desktop

My Documents

My Computer

My Network

File name: Chapter 1

Files of type: All picture files

Save

Cancel

Put a name for the file here.

To find work you have saved, click on the "Open" button. This opens a **window**. The window helps you find your file.

Sometimes we save files on other machines, such as music players.

Activity

Go to a computer and write some words in a word processor **program**. Save the file and close the word processor window. Can you find the file and open it again?

Following Instructions

A computer needs a list of instructions to tell it what to do. A computer **program**, such as a word processor or painting program, is a list of instructions. The computer follows the instructions.

The computer follows a program so that you can play a game.

Changing the program makes a computer do a different job. We can make a computer do almost any job we like, from playing games to flying an aircraft.

Looking Inside

This is what we would see if we could look inside a computer.

This is a motherboard. Most parts of the computer are attached to this board.

Memory chips remember information when the computer is switched on.

fan

Computers are made up of many parts that work together. Computers help us work much more quickly and easily. We can have a lot of fun using computers!

The processor is like the computer's brain. It does calculations and moves information around in the memory. It can do millions of sums in a second.

STAY SAFE ☒

⚠ Never open a computer case. You could break the small parts inside, and the electricity could hurt you.

Fun Facts About Computers

- The first computers were huge. One computer could fill a whole room.

- The first **mouse** was invented in 1964. It was made of wood and had two metal wheels.

Find Out More

Ashley, Susan. *I Can Use a Computer*. Milwaukee, WI: Gareth Stevens, 2005.

Dubois, Muriel L. *I Like Computers: What Can I Be?* Mankato, MN: Capstone, 2005.

Glossary

data information that you put into a computer

desktop area on a computer screen showing folders and programs

digital camera camera that takes photographs that can be put onto a computer

icon small picture on a computer screen

menu list of choices that are shown on a computer screen

mouse tool attached to a computer, used to point and click on the screen

program set of instructions that tells a computer what to do

window box on the screen that gives you a choice of what to do

Index